ROMANTIC DELICACIES

PHOTOGRAPHY AND DESIGN
BY KOREN TRYGG
TEXT BY LUCY POSHEK

ANTIOCH GOURMET
GIFT BOOKS

Published by Antioch Publishing Company
Yellow Springs, Ohio 45387

ISBN 0-89954-831-8

ROMANTIC DELICACIES

Printed and bound in the U.S.A.

CONTENTS

A HISTORY OF ROMANTIC FOODS

Since the dawn of romance we have been pursuing the mysterious connection between food and love. Why do certain delicacies have such seductive properties? Is there really such a thing as an aphrodisiac? What *are* romantic foods?

The word *aphrodisiac* is derived from Aphrodite, the Greek goddess of love and fertility, who was born from the foaming sea. The ancient Greeks built temples dedicated to Aphrodite and worshipped any food relating to her. Like her son, Eros, and Venus—her Roman counterpart—Aphrodite represented affection, lust and sex.

Eventually the word *aphrodisiac* came to mean any food that awakened desire, whether by its symbolic nature, energizing content, or pure sensuality. Consequently, almost every food, herb and spice was viewed as a stimulant at one time or another even if it was offensive, dangerous, or downright poisonous. For example, onions, garlic and leeks were highly regarded by the ancients as foods of love. Emperor Nero ate so many leeks to improve his prowess that he was nicknamed the "leek-eater."

Other civilizations treasured aphrodisiacs long before the word even existed. The Chinese tradition of exotic love potions dates back millenniums. Eels were considered gods among the Egyptian love foods. The Indians and Arabs

attached a mystique to spices, eggs and fruit by extolling their magical powers in literature such as the *Kama Sutra* and *Arabian Nights*. And chocolate—believed by the Aztecs to increase one's passion—was consumed by Montezuma's court at the rate of two thousand cups a day.

Love potions, or philters, reached their peak of popularity during the Middle Ages, when all kinds of bizarre concoctions were plied on peasants and royalty alike. Some foods were thought to be so stimulative by medieval society that they were banned. The monks, for instance, were forbidden to grow any "herbs of love," such as summer savory, in their gardens.

Henry VIII, who had a voracious appetite for both food and wives, often consumed candied flowers in the belief that they enhanced his ardor. Carrots were common ingredients in Elizabethan love elixirs. Invigorating potions were also widely used at Louis XIV's court. The Duc de Richelieu, a contemporary of Casanova, hosted meals at which everyone dined *au naturel* on oysters and marzipan. Madame Pompadour—mistress to Louis XV—always ate fillet of sole, truffles and chocolate prior to her royal trysts.

Although the legends surrounding some of the more bizarre aphrodisiacs have long since been dispelled, modern research has unveiled a close connection between certain foods and amorous impulses. For one thing, our romantic desires and our appetites for food and drink begin in the same part of the brain—in the hypothalamus. When we crave certain tastes, such as sweetness, it is because they are closest to the pleasure centers of our minds.

Any foods that give the body quick energy—including fresh fruits and vegetables—can also be considered aphrodisiacs. Anything that awakens the central nervous system or promotes blood circulation falls into this category, too. This means that besides invigorating substances such as ginseng, cocoa and tea, general fitness and good health can be a natural contributor to one's romantic sparkle.

Other foods are considered aphrodisiacs because they affect the arousal hormones. Phosphorus is the number-one mineral linked to these hormones. Best consumed in moderate amounts, its sources are seafood, eggs, milk, nuts, seeds and beans.

Certain comestibles, such as sinfully expensive chocolates and champagne, are romantic for their sentiment and extravagance as well as their consuming pleasures. Other foods not only have sensual appeal but also spark a delightful sense of anticipation—a vital key to the serious art of seduction.

No matter how you look at it, romantic delicacies play a natural role in love—because, above all, you can share them together.

"After a perfect meal we are more susceptible to the ecstasy of love than at any other time."

DR. HANS BAZLI

SETTING THE MOOD

Cooking for your true love is one of the most romantic gestures possible. But there are many ways to add alluring warmth to the scene that go beyond mere culinary skills. The extra touches behind a seductive meal may be only subliminal details; but love is often found in the details.

—Flowers are a beautiful, sentimental, fragrant, and sometimes even edible stimulus to a romantic repast. For centuries, they have been considered an integral part of courtship. The Romans regarded jasmine and roses as tokens of love. Tuberoses not only fill the room with a luscious tropical scent, but they also symbolize forbidden pleasures. Other symbolic flowers include everlastings, artemisia and orchids. You can go minimalist with a single bud vase or go wild with big bouquets—but make sure you can see each other across the table!

—Set your table with care and elegance—pretty plates, silverware and glasses. Place your sauces in nice bowls— no plastic containers. Always use large cloth napkins rather than paper napkins—even at a picnic. Hide a little love note inside the folded napkin of your sweetheart.

—It almost goes without saying—for an intimate supper or dinner, turn the lights low, low, low. Illuminate the room with lots of flickering candles, or a cozy crackling fire to snuggle up to.

—Relaxing, sensuous music is a must. If in doubt, put on romantic classical piano, Spanish classical guitar, sexy Brazilian bossa novas, or soft jazz—nothing too pensive, heavy or loud. Among the most romantic classical composers are Chopin, Vivaldi, Schumann, Puccini, and Granados; for twentieth-century romance, try Billie Holiday, Edith Piaf, Antonio Carlos Jobim, or Miles Davis. If you want to be boldly flirtatious, put on Ravel's "Bolero," Rimsky-Korsakov's "Scheherazade," or some wicked tangos.

—Prepare most of your meal in advance so you won't have to rush around or worry about something going wrong at the last minute. Nervous excitement is one thing; tension will spoil the mood of the whole occasion.

—Alcohol—particularly champagne—does much to lift inhibitions and make an occasion special. Robert Louis Stevenson aptly called wine "bottled poetry." On the other hand, as Mr. Shakespeare pointed out, overindulgence in alcohol may "provoketh desire but takes away the performance." Try not to exceed more than two glasses of wine and maybe an after-dinner liqueur. Think of a romantic toast to accompany your first drink.

—Keep your entrées light, portions small, and you will feel one hundred percent more energetic after the meal. And if you wish to cook with onions, garlic, or hot peppers, make sure you have the consent of your partner.

The care spent on an amorous ambience and a sensual table is a basic ingredient of love and will help ensure a lusty appetite in your special someone.

BREAKFAST IN BED

There's nothing quite so decadent as having breakfast in bed with the one you love, lingering all morning over big cups of frothy cappuccino and an energizing breakfast.

For a different twist, steam some chocolate milk for your cappuccino and add chocolate chips to your muffins. The seductive powers of chocolate have been praised since ancient times. Indeed, scientists have recently unearthed a substance in chocolate that contains the same chemical produced in the brain when people fall in love. This, plus its mineral and caffeine content, may explain why chocolate can make one feel quite giddy at times.

Whip up an omelet with some French cheese, herbs of love, and exotic mushrooms thrown in. Mushrooms are mentioned in the romantic cookery lore of almost every country.

For centuries, fruits have been considered aphrodisiacs. Not only do they offer a succulent taste and juiciness but they also contain natural vitamins and sugars. The most traditional love fruits include pineapples, mangos, papayas, figs, pomegranates, peaches, apricots and bananas.

A bowl of tropical fruit would be the perfect complement to an enticing breakfast in bed. Top the fruit with some fresh mint leaves (used by the Arabs to enhance

one's prowess). Pour a bit of vitamin C-laden orange juice into glasses half-filled with champagne; garnish the mimosa with a bit of passion fruit and see what kind of fun ensues.

Arrange your breakfast attractively on a tray with big cloth French napkins and a single bud vase with a rose or orchid. Accompany your entry with Puccini's aria, "*O mio babbino caro,*" or "*L'amour est un oiseau rebelle*" from Bizet's *Carmen* . . . in which case the rose should be between your teeth.

"*B*urgundy makes you think of silly things;
Bordeaux makes you talk about them;
and Champagne makes you do them.*"*

BRILLAT-SAVARIN

MENU

Casanova's Cappuccino
Orange Chocolate-Chip Muffins
Wild Mushroom Omelet
Fresh Tropical Fruits
Mimosa

Casanova's Cappuccino

Have ready equal amounts of hot espresso and hot steamed chocolate milk. Pour equal parts coffee and milk into coffee cups. Sprinkle with cinnamon.

Orange Chocolate-Chip Muffins

¾ cup (6 fl. oz.) milk
½ cup (4 fl. oz.) oil
2 eggs
1 tsp. (¾ Br. tsp.) vanilla extract
½ tsp. orange extract
4 tsp. (3 Br. tsp.) freshly grated orange peel
2 cups (16 fl. oz.) all-purpose flour
1 cup (8 fl. oz.) oatmeal
⅓ cup (2⅔ fl. oz.) brown sugar
2 tsp. (1½ Br. tsp.) baking powder
1 tsp. (¾ Br. tsp.) cinnamon
1 tsp. (¾ Br. tsp.) salt
½ tsp. ground ginger
⅔ cup (5⅓ fl. oz.) chocolate chips

Preheat oven to 400°F. Grease 12 muffin cups. Beat wet ingredients together in a mixing bowl. In a separate bowl, combine dry ingredients. Blend wet and dry ingredients together, stirring until just moistened. Fold in chocolate chips. Spoon batter into prepared pan, filling each cup nearly full. Bake about 18 minutes or until inserted toothpick comes out clean.

Wild Mushroom Omelet

1 cup (8 fl. oz.) sliced raw mushrooms or reconstituted dry
   mushrooms (try chanterelle, crimi, shiitake, or white, in
   any combination)
3 tbsp. (2¼ Br. tbsp.) butter
1 clove garlic, peeled and halved
2 sprigs fresh savory
4 eggs
2 tbsp. (1½ Br. tbsp.) water
salt and pepper
2–3 oz. Camembert cheese, rind removed, cut into pieces

In a skillet over medium heat, melt 1 tbsp. (¾ Br. tbsp.) butter. Add the garlic and savory, then the mushrooms. Cook, stirring constantly until the mushrooms are tender. Spoon mushrooms into a small bowl lined with paper towel to absorb excess moisture; remove garlic and savory. Return skillet to medium heat and melt 2 tbsp. (1½ Br. tbsp.) butter. Meanwhile, beat the eggs with the water. Add salt and pepper as desired. Pour eggs into prepared skillet. When the eggs are almost set, add the cheese to half the omelet, then add the mushrooms on top of the cheese. Cook until the cheese just starts to melt, about 1 minute. Fold the omelet and slide onto a plate. Serves 2.

A PROVOCATIVE PICNIC

The sun itself can be an aphrodisiac on warm lazy days, drawing lovers outside for their culinary rendezvous. There is no end to the romantic settings you could select for a picnic. A country meadow, or a park, or the beach are the most traditional choices. If you really want to make this an occasion, how about a gondola, or balloon, or horse carriage ride? And what about right outside your door? On your rooftop? The fire escape? Even if it rains, you can spread a quilt on the floor, put on some sounds of nature, and enjoy your picnic right in your own living room.

Finger food is not only the most practical picnic food, but very sensual as well. Without having to balance a plate on your lap, you will be free to recline and enjoy your delicacies Roman style. Nibble on little morsels of crusty French bread spread with creamy cheese while sipping a favorite vintage of champagne; swirl some tender prawns or artichoke leaves in a delectable sauce. Take a strawberry by its stem, dip it into your champagne, or a bowl of thick cream, or sugar, and feed it to your lover. In fact, if the day is hot enough, fruit may be all you need for a provocative picnic.

MENU

Tortas d'Amore
Crusty French Bread
Prawns of Venus
Steamy Artichokes with French Dip
Fresh Ripe Strawberries
Champagne

Tortas d'Amore

Tortas can be made with any combination of softened cheeses, herbs, and nut fillings.

To make two different *tortas*: line a small heart-shaped dish and a small soufflé dish (each one 3 to 4 inches in diameter) with 2 layers of dampened cheesecloth in each, leaving enough to cover tops. Prepare the following fillings:

−Blend together ½ cup (4 fl. oz.) softened Gorgonzola cheese and ⅓ cup (2⅔ fl. oz.) softened cream cheese.

−Blend together ⅓ cup (2 ⅔ fl. oz.) softened cream cheese and ⅓ cup (2 ⅔ fl. oz.) softened unsalted butter.

−Purée together ½ cup (4 fl. oz.) fresh basil leaves, firmly packed, with 1 tbsp. (¾ Br. tbsp.) extra virgin olive oil, 2 tsp. (1½ Br. tsp.) lightly toasted pine nuts, 1 tsp. (¾ Br. tsp.) freshly grated Parmesan cheese, and salt to taste.

−2 tbsp. (1½ Br. tbsp.) marinated sun-dried tomatoes, finely chopped.

−2 tbsp. (1½ Br. tbsp.) whole pine nuts, lightly toasted.

In the bottom of the heart-shaped dish, first layer the sun-dried tomatoes, then a cream cheese layer, pesto, and end with another cream cheese layer.

In the bottom of the soufflé dish, place a few fresh basil leaves or edible flowers. Add a layer of Gorgonzola, pine nuts, cream cheese, pesto, more Gorgonzola, pine nuts, cream cheese, pesto, and end with a final layer of Gorgonzola.

Fold the cheesecloth over the tops of the tortas. *Refrigerate at least 2 hours. Unmold onto serving plates, removing cheesecloth. Serve at room temperature.*

Prawns of Venus

10 large prawns, raw and unpeeled
3 cups (24 fl. oz.) water
3 cups (24 fl. oz.) champagne or dry white wine
½ cup (4 fl. oz.) celery, chopped
1 bay leaf
1 tbsp. (¾ Br. tbsp.) fresh lemon juice
¼ tsp. black peppercorns
dash of salt

Place all ingredients except prawns in a medium saucepan. Bring to a boil. Let liquid cook 2 minutes; then add prawns and reduce heat to a simmer, cooking 3 to 5 minutes until prawns turn pink and are cooked. Remove from heat and place cooked prawns on ice to cool. When cool, remove shells, leaving tails attached. Cover and refrigerate. Serve with French Dip.

"The artichoke above all is a vegetable expression of civilized living, of the long view, of increasing delight by anticipation and crescendo. No wonder it was once regarded as an aphrodisiac."

JANE GRIGSON

Steamy Artichokes with French Dip

Trim and steam whole artichokes, adding the juice of 1 whole lemon to the water to prevent discoloration. Drain and chill. Serve with French Dip.

French Dip

1 cup (8 fl. oz.) mayonnaise
4 tbsp. (3 Br. tbsp.) chutney
2 tsp. (1½ Br. tsp.) lemon juice
½ tsp. cayenne pepper
½ tsp. Worcestershire sauce
¼ tsp. Tabasco sauce

Combine all ingredients. Chill until ready to serve.

*"What better way to win a heart
than to spend a lazy summer afternoon
in some shady and secluded country spot,
a stream meandering by at the foot of the grassy
slope, a few fleecy clouds floating overhead, and a
bright red-and-white checkered cloth spread out,
upon which sits the champagne, the fat wedge of
pâté de campagne, the strawberries and cream?"*

JOHN THORNE

A SEDUCTIVE SUPPER

Since shellfish are some of
the strongest aphrodisiacs—rich in phosphorus, iodine and
vitamins—what could be more seductive than a sexy sea-

food supper? Tie oversized napkins around your necks and eat the shellfish with your hands. Put on some sensual music and re-enact the notorious eating scene from the film *Tom Jones*. A finger bowl scented with lemon will freshen your hands afterwards.

Oysters, the king of love foods, were praised by Pliny as "the palm and pleasure of the table." Casanova consumed no less than fifty oysters a day. Best served as an appetizer, they are most potent when eaten raw and plain with a little lemon juice on a plate of crushed ice. Accompany them with a crisp dry champagne and you will soon be overcome with bliss.

Bouillabaisse—a divine shellfish stew—was reputedly enjoyed by Venus as a restorative after her strenuous affairs with Mars. According to legend she gave the recipe to the fishermen of Marseilles over two thousand years ago. The Marseillais still put in a wide variety of fish—but only those that are very fresh and readily available. A *rouille*, or spicy sauce, is usually spooned into the middle of the soup to give it added richness. A thick slice of bread, such as Italian focaccia, is the perfect dipping tool for the broth. Garnish the bread with rosemary leaves— also said to be a stimulant.

To further enhance your evening of pleasure, prepare a simple Caesar salad, which features two other mild aphrodisiacs—raw eggs and anchovies. The old Arab and French love potions often called for raw egg yolks in the belief that they travelled straight into the bloodstream. Although high in fats, they also contain a great deal of

protein and minerals.

As the finale to your intimate supper, consider a love elixir of zabaglione and soft ripe fruit. Consumed by the Italians since Renaissance times, zabaglione is both rich and exhilarating.

*"Great food is like great sex.
The more you have, the more you want."*

GAEL GREENE

MENU

*Oysters on the Half Shell
Caesar & Cleopatra Salad
Bouillabaisse of Love
Rosemary Focaccia
Zabaglione with Fresh Fruit
Red Wine*

Caesar & Cleopatra Salad

1 garlic clove, cut in half
1 egg
juice of ½ lemon
½ tsp. Worcestershire sauce
½ tsp. Dijon mustard
¼ tsp. each salt & freshly ground black pepper
¼ cup (2 fl. oz.) olive oil
½ bunch romaine, torn into bite-size pieces
½ avocado, peeled and sliced
¼ lb. mushrooms, sliced
2 tbsp. (1½ Br. tbsp.) grated Parmesan cheese
½ cup (4 fl. oz.) croutons
anchovies (opt.)

Rub a wooden salad bowl with the garlic clove. In a blender, combine egg, lemon juice, Worcestershire, mustard, salt and pepper (garlic clove optional). While blender is running, add oil in a thin stream until dressing thickens. (Can refrigerate until ready to use.) In the prepared salad bowl, toss the romaine leaves with dressing until well coated. Add avocado, mushrooms, grated cheese, croutons, and anchovies, tossing again. Serves 2.

To make your own croutons: Brush cubed French bread (crusts removed) with olive oil and sprinkle with herbs. Bake on a cookie sheet at 300°F until golden brown.

Bouillabaisse of Love

1 lb. clams or mussels
1 lb. lobster dainties or crab claws
½ lb. shrimp
¼ lb. scallops or sea bass
¼ cup (2 fl. oz.) olive oil
½ cup (4 fl. oz.) fresh fennel, chopped
1 8-oz. can stewed tomatoes
½ of a 6-oz. can tomato paste
1 tbsp. (¾ Br. tbsp.) lemon juice
2-3 bay leaves
½ tsp. fennel seeds
¼ tsp. salt
¼ tsp. saffron (opt.)
zest from ½ orange
dash of cayenne pepper

Rouille
2 tbsp. (1½ Br. tbsp.) mayonnaise
1 tsp. (¾ Br. tsp.) paprika
1 tsp. (¾ Br. tsp.) lemon juice
dash of cayenne pepper

Wash fish and scrub shellfish well. Heat olive oil in a stockpot; add chopped fennel and sauté until tender. Add 3 cups (24 fl. oz.) water, fish, shellfish, and remaining ingredients. Simmer for 10-15 minutes.

Meanwhile, stir the rouille ingredients together in

a small bowl and set aside.

When bouillabaisse is ready, swirl a circle of rouille in the bottoms of 2 serving bowls; place a variety of shellfish in each bowl; then add the broth. Serves 2.

Zabaglione with Fresh Fruit

4 egg yolks
3 tbsp. (2¼ Br. tbsp.) sugar
¼ cup (2 fl. oz.) marsala wine
fresh sliced peaches or pears

In the top pan of a double boiler, mix egg yolks and sugar with an electric mixer for 2 minutes. Slowly beat in the marsala. Place pan over hot (not boiling) water, continually beating with electric mixer until custard has thickened and holds its shape, about 5 minutes. Serve warm or chilled in dessert glasses with slices of fresh peaches or pears. Serves 2.

*"One cannot think well, love well, sleep well,
if one has not dined well."*

VIRGINIA WOOLF

A Valentine's Dinner

F or Valentine's Day, anniversaries or any other romantic occasion, it's time to shoot Cupid's arrow and pull out all the stops. The table should

be positively swooning with flowers, lace, romantic red, and hearts.

This does not mean you have to spend hours in the kitchen; you have better things to do with your sweetheart. But your dinner should be artfully arranged and full of sentimental tokens. Buy pasta in fancifully-shaped bow ties or hearts. Arrange your food in creative heart shapes with red accents: This can be as simple as curving two pink shrimps towards each other, tails meeting; or as elaborate as a rich, homemade, heart-shaped chocolate cake laden with liqueur and red raspberries.

Caviar—easy to digest and ultrahigh in phosphorus, calcium and protein—is the classic appetizer of love. Once reserved for royalty, the delicacy was fervently consumed by such kings such as Alexander the Great, the Austro-Hungarian emperors, and Russian czars. Of course, James Bond's favorite kind of caviar was Beluga.

If you are serving meat with your special dinner, try to have it sliced thinly—easier to digest. Among the tastier, more versatile meats are pastrami, ham, and prosciutto.

Any flowers enhance the romantic atmosphere, but some have long been considered aphrodisiacs when eaten, too. Since most edible flowers haven't much of a flavor aside from a slight bitterness or perfumed sweetness, their value may be more subliminal—in their pleasing shapes and colors. According to the ancients, a few of the most seductive edible flowers include wild violets, marigolds, pansies, rose petals (rose water was used in many love potions), lemon verbena, and wild orchid bulbs (now

very scarce).

If you're looking for an edible red accent for your dishes, try bergamot, rose petals, red nasturtiums, or the flowers of pineapple sage. Be sure the flowers are pesticide-free. Many markets and herbalists now carry edible flowers. Use them as a garnish for salads, fruits, sorbets and any light entrées.

No Valentine's dinner would be complete without a dessert of rich dark chocolate—the universal food of romance. One may derive complete pleasure from its taste alone. But chocolate is also known to contain a chemical, nicknamed "the love drug," which is the same substance present in the brain when love strikes. It's no wonder then, that chocolate has left a luscious trail of romantic tradition.

Decorate your table with candles, rosebuds tied to the napkins with a ribbon, and, at your sweetheart's place setting, a traditional valentine, *billet-doux*, or other little sentiment. The custom of valentine cards dates back to the eighteenth century. The heart shape—the classic symbol of love—can now be carried beyond cards in many creative culinary ways.

It is believed that the custom of Valentine's Day has roots not in Saint Valentine but in a medieval belief that birds choose their mates around mid-February.

MENU

Heart-Shaped Hors d'Oeuvres
Passionate Pasta
Aphrodite's Salad
White Wine
Dark Chocolate-Raspberry Torte
After-Dinner Brandy

Heart-Shaped Hors d'Oeuvres

With a simple heart-shaped cookie cutter you can create an endless variety of valentine hors d'oeuvres from breads, tortillas, jicama—you name it.

Heart-shaped sandwiches: Spread thin slices of firm bread (white, wheat or pumpernickel work well—toasted or untoasted) with softened, flavored butter, mayonnaise, pâté, or creamy cheese. Avoiding the crusts, cut hearts out of the slices with the cookie cutter. Garnish each heart with a sumptuous delicacy.

Suggested toppings: Red radishes and watercress on herbed butter; asparagus tips and pimento on lemon mayonnaise; sliced Roma tomatoes and basil leaves on fresh mozzarella drizzled with olive oil; smoked salmon and capers, or prosciutto and sliced figs, on cream cheese; sun-dried tomatoes on a purée of black olives, olive oil, and garlic; smoked oysters on creamy Gorgonzola; red caviar and fresh dill on toast; sliced strawberries on fruit-flavored cream cheese.

Other Heart-Shaped Appetizers

—Melt grated cheese between two large flour tortillas; cut the quesadilla into heart shapes and garnish each heart with guacamole and sour cream or red salsa.

—Cut a thin-crusted baked pizza into hearts (avoiding the outside crust) and serve hot.

—Cut heart shapes from thinly sliced jicama. Place a red nasturtium flower on each heart and fill the flowers with sour cream and black caviar.

Passionate Pasta

6-8 oz. fancifully-shaped pasta, cooked
3 tbsp. (2¼ Br. tbsp.) olive oil
¼ lb. thinly sliced prosciutto
8-10 black pitted olives
8 artichoke hearts, canned or frozen (well drained)
1 tbsp. (¾ Br. tbsp.) capers
½ tsp. crushed red peppers
1 cup (8 fl. oz.) light cream
grated Parmesan or Romano cheese

In a skillet on medium heat, briefly sauté prosciutto in 1 tbsp. (¾ Br. tbsp.) olive oil. Remove from pan and set aside. Add remaining olive oil to the skillet and briefly heat olives, artichoke hearts, and capers. Add red peppers and light cream. Stir until mixture bubbles and thickens slightly; then add the cooked pasta and prosciutto, stirring until well coated. Before serving, sprinkle grated Parmesan or Romano cheese on top. Serves 2.

Aphrodite's Salad

Place one or two Greek grape leaves or several blanched spinach leaves on two salad plates. Arrange ripe red tomato slices, asparagus tips, and hearts of palm on top of the leaves. Sprinkle lightly with vinaigrette dressing. Garnish with edible flowers if desired.

Dark Chocolate-Raspberry Torte

Torte

4 oz. semisweet chocolate
2 tbsp. (1½ Br. tbsp.) crème de cacao or amaretto
¼ lb. softened butter
¾ cup (6 fl. oz.) sugar
4 medium eggs, separated
¼ tsp. almond extract (if using amaretto)
¼ tsp. vanilla extract
¼ cup (2 fl. oz.) dry bread crumbs
½ cup (4 fl. oz.) flour

Glaze

1 oz. semisweet chocolate
1 tbsp. (¾ Br. tbsp.) crème de cacao or amaretto
3 tbsp. (2¼ Br. tbsp.) butter
1 cup (8 fl. oz.) fresh raspberries

Preheat oven to 350°F. Butter and flour one 8-inch heart-shaped or round cake pan, placing a piece of wax paper in the bottom.

In a double boiler over hot water, melt and stir the chocolate and liqueur together. In a mixing bowl, cream the butter, sugar and egg yolks together. Add the melted chocolate, vanilla and almond extracts to the butter mixture.

In another mixing bowl, beat the egg whites until soft peaks form. Fold a quarter of the egg whites into the chocolate batter. Then, working quickly, fold in

the remaining egg whites, alternating with the flour and bread crumbs. Pour batter into cake pan. Bake for 20 to 25 minutes. Torte is done when a toothpick comes clean from the outside perimeter but slightly oily from the center. Cool on wire racks; then turn onto a flat serving plate.

Meanwhile melt the chocolate square, butter and liqueur in a double boiler over hot water; stir until smooth. Beat in butter a bit at a time. When glaze has cooled, spread over the top of the torte.

This torte can be prepared one day ahead and refrigerated—in fact, its texture is even better after a day. Just before serving, garnish the top of torte and border the plate with fresh raspberries. (Marinate them in crème de cacao or amaretto first, if desired.)

GIFTS FROM THE HEART

There are plenty of ready-made edible gifts you can give to your loved one. But why not treat your sweetie to a homemade gift from the heart, such as rich, liqueur-laced truffles, chocolate-dipped fruit, or herbs of love immersed in aromatic oils and vinegars? The gesture will be far more meaningful than the most extravagant box of store-bought chocolates.

Present your edible gifts with stylish touches: Wrap a few of your homemade confections in clear, sparkly, cellophane tied with a ribbon; preserve your herbal oils in a beautiful bottle trimmed with raffia string.

Other edible gifts from the heart:

—Take your trusty heart-shaped cookie cutter and create hearts from shortbread dough or baked brownies.

—If the two of you are sharing a favorite movie, pop some popcorn and flavor it with spicy spices: Melt the butter together with dashes of Worcestershire sauce, salt, cinnamon, cayenne pepper, and Tabasco sauce, as desired; toss well.

—Assemble a pretty gift basket filled with exotic tropical fruits, soft summer fruits, or berries.

—Give your sweetheart a little pot of basil—a token of love in Italy.

"A man taking basil from a woman will love her always."
SIR THOMAS MORE

Chocolate-Dipped Strawberries

Wash fresh whole strawberries, stems intact, and drain them on paper towels. Cut a bar of fine-quality milk chocolate or semisweet dipping chocolate into bits. Melt the chocolate in the top of a double boiler, stirring frequently. Remove pan from heat. Dip strawberries, one by one, in the melted chocolate. Cool them on a sheet of foil. Store dipped strawberries in a covered container in the refrigerator until ready to serve. Best eaten the same day.

Note: Some stores now sell dipping chocolate in a jar that you can heat up directly in the microwave.

Grand Marnier Truffles

4 oz. fine-quality semisweet chocolate, broken into bits
3 tbsp. (2¼ Br. tbsp.) heavy cream
1 tbsp. (¾ Br. tbsp.) powdered (icing) sugar
1 tbsp. (¾ Br. tbsp.) Grand Marnier or orange liqueur
2 tbsp. (1½ Br. tbsp.) unsweetened cocoa powder

In a small dry saucepan over very low heat, melt chocolate with heavy cream, stirring until smooth. Pour mixture into a mixing bowl. Add powdered sugar and beat with an electric mixer for 8 minutes until thick. Add liqueur and beat 2 minutes longer. Cover and chill.

Shape chocolate into ½-inch balls. Roll in unsweetened cocoa powder to coat. Refrigerate or freeze until ready to serve.

Cheesecake Heartlets

1 cup (8 fl. oz.) chocolate wafers, crumbled
4 tbsp. (3 Br. tbsp.) unsalted butter, melted
1 8-oz. package cream cheese, softened
¼ tsp. vanilla extract
⅓ cup (2⅔ fl. oz.) sugar
1 egg
⅓ cup (2⅔ fl. oz.) semisweet chocolate chips
  (mini-size, if available)

*C*ombine wafer crumbs and butter. Press in bottom
and sides of three 5-inch heart-shaped or round tartlet
pans.

   Preheat oven to 350°F. In a medium mixing bowl,
beat cream cheese and vanilla with an electric mixer
until fluffy. Gradually beat in sugar. Add egg and mix
well. Fold in the chocolate chips. Pour mixture into
prepared tartlet pans. Place pans on a cookie sheet.
Bake 25 to 30 minutes until cheesecake begins to
crack at edges and the center is firm. Remove from
oven and cool. Chill thoroughly, ideally overnight.
Remove from pans when ready to serve.

*"T*here is no love sincerer than the love of food."*
GEORGE BERNARD SHAW

Gourmet Oils & Vinegars

Rosemary Oil: 4 fresh rosemary sprigs
                     2 garlic cloves
                     2 cups (16 fl. oz.) extra virgin olive oil

Basil Oil: 10 fresh basil leaves
                     2 cups (16 fl. oz.) extra virgin olive oil

Sage Vinegar: 4 fresh sage sprigs
                     2 cups (16 fl. oz.) white wine vinegar

Oregano Vinegar: 4 fresh oregano sprigs
                     2 cups (16 fl. oz.) white wine vinegar

Fill a bottle with herbs and liquid. Place in a sunny spot for 2 to 4 weeks, shaking now and then.

LOVE POTIONS

Love potions and powders date back to ancient times when it was believed that they could not only increase one's ardor but also cause a person to fall helplessly in love. Needless to say, no potion has been found to accomplish this feat entirely on its own. But there are special concoctions that have been known to produce a noticeable sensation of vigor.

Recipes for love potions have survived centuries of folklore. Almost every herb, spice and flower figured heavily in these potions at one time or another. According to an old Middle Eastern recipe, a man who consumes chick pea nectar every morning will be able to "enjoy a hundred women." An ancient Druid tonic called for chervil, heather, honeysuckle, red clover, and vervain—a plant sacred to Venus. A fourteenth-century cookbook written for Richard II recommended many bizarre ingredients for love potions; one of its more orthodox recipes included rose petals, almond milk, cinnamon, ginger, rice flour, fresh dates, and pine kernels. A seventeenth-century powder contained cinnamon, ginger, thyme, rosemary, grated nutmeg, and galingale root.

Chinese love potions frequently included ginseng syrup, royal jelly, and a wide variety of exotic herbs that are still largely unknown in the Western world. Fresh

ginger—known to stimulate the circulation—has also been revered as a Chinese aphrodisiac for over three thousand years.

Ginseng is derived from an Asian plant root. In the first *Chinese materia medica*, written over two thousand years ago, the author noted that ginseng, "if taken for some time will invigorate the body and prolong life." Today it is still thought to maintain balance of the mind and spirit as well as the body. It is one of the few foods which have been found by scientists to produce a positive increase in physical and mental energy, in addition to an overall sense of well being when taken on a regular basis. Various forms of ginseng are sold in most health food stores—most popularly as a liquid extract. Ginseng should not be consumed in large quantities, or continually for more than three months—stick to the recommended doses.

Possessing both a sweet and slightly bitter flavor, ginseng makes a good base for a "home-brewed" love potion. Try mixing it with various juices, nectars, spices and natural sweeteners.

"Straight to the 'pothecary's shop I went and in love powder all my money spent."

JOHN GAY

Love Potion #34

½ cup (4 fl. oz.) apricot nectar
1 tbsp. (¾ Br. tbsp.) ginseng
1 tsp. (¾ Br. tsp.) honey
½ tsp. chopped fresh ginger
dash of ground cinnamon

In a food processor, blend all ingredients until ginger is thoroughly puréed. Pour into a small glass. Serves 1.

*"Cooking is like love.
It should be entered into with abandon
or not at all."*

HARRIET VAN HORNE

GRAPHIC DESIGN BY GRETCHEN GOLDIE

PHOTO STYLING BY SUE TALLON

ACKNOWLEDGMENTS

RAY AROMATORIO AND KIM KONOPKA, DAVID GOETZ,
LINDA LAMPSON AND MARK MEIERDING,
WILLIAM H. MEIERDING,
JOE POSHEK, KIRK SAND,
CHARLES AND JULIETTE TRYGG